KU-337-340

Schools Library and Information Services
S00000681726

Elizabeth Raum

www.raintreepublishers.co.uk
Visit our website to find out more information about **Raintree** books.

To order:

Phone 44 (0) 1865 888112
Send a fax to 44 (0) 1865 314091
Visit the Raintree bookshop at **www.raintreepublishers.co.uk** to browse our catalogue and order online.

First published in Great Britain by Raintree, Halley Court, Jordan Hill, Oxford OX2 8EJ, part of Harcourt Education. Raintree is a registered trademark of Harcourt Education Ltd.

Editorial: Louise Galpine and Harriet Milles
Design: Victoria Bevan, Steve Mead, and Bigtop
Picture research: Mica Brancic and Hannah Taylor
Illustrations: Jeff Ward
Production: Julie Carter

Originated by Chroma Graphics Pte. Ltd
Printed and bound in China by Leo Paper Group

ISBN 978 1 4062 0688 3 (hardback)
12 11 10 09 08
10 9 8 7 6 5 4 3 2 1

ISBN 978 1 4062 0709 5 (paperback)
12 11 10 09 08
10 9 8 7 6 5 4 3 2 1

British Library Cataloguing in Publication Data
Raum, Elizabeth
Leaders. - (Atomic)
920'.02
A full catalogue record for this book is available from the British Library.

Acknowledgements
The publishers would like to thank the following for permission to reproduce photographs: The Art Archive/Museo del Prado Madrid/Dagli Orti p. **12**; akg-images p. **10**; Alamy Images/Ferruccio p. **29**; Corbis pp. **5**, **6**, **8**, **23**, **25** (Bettmann), **9** (Gianni Dagli Orti), **13** (Brooklyn Museum), **14** (Stefano Bianchetti), **16–17** (Christie's Images), **18** (Archivo Iconografico, S.A.), **22** (Hulton-Deutsch Collection), **26–27**; Getty Images/AFP p. **21**.

Cover photograph of a bust of Julius Caesar reproduced by permission of Getty Images/Time Life Pictures.

The publishers would like to thank Nancy Harris, Diana Bentley, and Dee Reid for their assistance in the preparation of this book.

Contents

Some words are printed in bold, **like this**. You can find out what they mean in the glossary. You can also look in the box at the bottom of the page where the word first appears.

Julius Caesar (100 BC–44 BC)

World leaders have changed our world, for better or worse. Should we judge them on the basis of their achievements? Or should we consider their character as well? Were these people heroes or villains? What makes a great leader? You decide.

Julius Caesar is one of the most famous leaders in history. Under Caesar's rule, the boundaries of the Roman **Empire** grew to cover much of southern Europe and sections of northern Africa. He marched throughout Europe and Asia, defeating his enemies and claiming territory for Rome.

The power of Rome

Caesar made Rome the most powerful empire on Earth. In 46 BC he was elected **dictator** for 10 years.

dictator	**ruler with absolute (unquestioned) power**
empire	**group of nations under the same ruler**

This image shows Caesar greeting his victorious Roman army.

The purple-coloured areas on this map show the Roman Empire in about 44 BC.

Caesar was stabbed to death by his own senators. His body was displayed to the public.

As Rome's dictator, Julius Caesar developed a new system of law. He built roads and libraries and developed the calendar that we use today. Caesar enjoyed power and personal glory.

Too powerful?

However, Caesar's thirst for power led people to fear him. He showed no mercy to the people he conquered, and turned millions of people into Roman slaves. As dictator, Caesar gave orders that he expected others to obey without question.

Even Rome's rich landowners feared Caesar. They worried that he would take away their wealth and power. A group of **senators** thought Caesar had become too powerful. On 15 March 44 BC, they stabbed Caesar to death.

Must leaders have a strong desire for power? Can only proud and **ambitious** people be strong leaders? What do you think?

ambitious — eagerly desiring success, power, and wealth

senator — (in ancient Rome) person who helped to make the laws

Joan of Arc (about 1412–1431)

In the early 1400s, a deeply religious 13-year-old French girl, Joan of Arc, saw bright visions and heard voices that told her she must save France.

Winning the French crown

Charles VII was supposed to be crowned king of France, but the English king, Henry VI, also wanted the crown. At the age of 17 Joan told her plan to Charles. Although Joan was poor and uneducated, Charles listened to her promise to help him become king. Charles gave Joan an army to attack France's English enemies. England was defeated and soon Charles VII became king of France.

At that time, women were expected to be wives and mothers, but Joan led soldiers into battle.

Joan's unselfish goals, religious faith, and love of France persuaded many others to follow her lead.

In 1429, Joan reclaimed the French town of Orléans from English soldiers.

Joan of Arc was sentenced to death by a French church court. She was about 19 years old when she died.

However, one year after Charles VII became king, Joan was captured and jailed by English soldiers. She was turned over to France for trial. A French priest who was loyal to the British condemned Joan of Arc to death by fire.

Deserted!

The French did not speak out on Joan's behalf. Her army deserted her. Even Charles VII was silent. At first, church leaders had praised Joan's religious faith. But then they became angry that Joan wore men's clothes and claimed that God spoke directly to her. They did not help her. She was killed by burning in 1431.

Joan of Arc's life as a leader lasted less than two years. What made people listen to her? Why did they later abandon her? Was Joan a hero?

Leading fact!

In 1920 the Roman Catholic Church made Joan of Arc a saint.

saint	**person recognized by the Catholic Church as having great holiness**

Queen Isabella

(1451–1504)

As a child in the 1400s, Princess Isabella of Castile (now in Spain) heard stories about Joan of Arc. Like Joan, Isabella grew up to be a deeply religious woman with strong ideas.

Equal power

Isabella refused to marry the man her father had chosen for her. Instead, she chose Ferdinand of Aragon (now in Spain). After they were married, Isabella and Ferdinand united their two countries into one strong Spanish nation. They ruled as equal partners.

Isabella brought prosperity, law, and order to Spain. She also supported exploration. Under her rule, Christopher Columbus sailed to the New World (now known as the Americas). Gradually, Spain became a world power.

Isabella's courage, intelligence, and beauty impressed the Spanish people.

Leading fact!

It took Columbus over six years to convince Queen Isabella and her advisors to give him the money to explore the New World.

This painting shows Christopher Columbus before Queen Isabella and King Ferdinand.

Isabella and Ferdinand are receiving a blessing from their chief inquisitor Tomás de Torquemada. They gave de Torquemada great power.

Isabella wanted to spread Christianity throughout the New World. Priests went to the Americas with explorers. Their mission was to **convert** native peoples into Christians.

The Inquisition

Isabella made some terrifying decisions. In Spain, Isabella appointed Tomás de Torquemada as the chief **inquisitor**. His job was to check people's religious beliefs. Anyone who was not Catholic was required to convert, or to leave Spain. Those who refused were tortured and killed.

Isabella changed Spain forever. Some of the changes did great good; others caused long-lasting harm. Some people say Isabella was right to impose her beliefs, but others say she was cruel and vicious. What do you think?

Leading fact!

During the Spanish Inquisition, between 160,000 and 180,000 Jewish people were driven out of Spain because they were not Christian.

convert	**change from one religion to another**
Inquisition	**search for non-believers**
inquisitor	**official investigator**

Napoleon Bonaparte

(1769–1821)

Napoleon Bonaparte was just a teenager when he joined the French army, but he quickly rose to power.

Making good laws

By 1795 Napoleon was a general and led troops to Italy, where they defeated the Austrian army. Then, he headed to Egypt with 35,000 men. After defeating the enemy there, Napoleon returned to France to take control of the French government.

Napoleon's government was based on his ideas of fairness and equality. Napoleon set up a fair tax system. A tax system is a method the government uses to collect money from its people to pay for public services. He allowed freedom of religion. He restored law and order through a strong police force. The **Napoleonic Code**, a system of law, was adopted in France and throughout Europe.

Napoleonic Code system of law based on Roman law

Napoleon achieved victory in Egypt in 1798. But his success did not last long. In 1801 his army was driven out of Egypt by the British.

Leading fact!

Throughout the years, people have said that Napoleon was short. He was actually about 1.6 metres (5 feet, 7 inches) tall – slightly taller than average for his day.

An artist painted Napoleon on a white stallion to make him appear heroic.

But then things began to go wrong. In June 1812 Napoleon led 611,000 troops into Russia. The French troops did not have the supplies needed to survive the cold conditions. By October only 40,000 soldiers were still alive. The survivors trudged home through the snow.

Surrender

Napoleon's enemies – Spain, Portugal, England, and Russia – joined together to defeat France. Sweden and Austria joined in, too. By 1814 France was broken and its armies were devastated. Napoleon surrendered and left France.

Napoleon tried to regain power at the Battle of Waterloo in 1815, but he lost there, too. He surrendered to the English on 15 July. Napoleon died in prison, on the tiny island of Saint Helena, six years later.

Consider Napoleon's leadership. Do you think he was a good leader? What led to his downfall?

Winston Churchill

(1874–1965)

Winston Churchill served Great Britain as a soldier and journalist. He was also a member of Parliament.

War!

During World War II (1939–1945), Churchill was the **prime minister**. He provided brilliant military and political leadership. He supervised the war efforts at home and was in charge of British military operations overseas. He travelled around the globe to consult with world leaders. His encouraging speeches inspired people everywhere. At the end of the war, he helped develop a peace **treaty**.

Leading fact!

In 1940 Churchill declared, "...we shall defend our island, whatever the cost may be, we shall fight on the beaches, we shall fight on the landing grounds, we shall fight in the fields and in the streets, we shall fight in the hills; we shall never surrender."

Churchill was known for this "V for victory" sign.

Parliament	group of elected people who make laws
prime minister	head of the government in a country with a parliament
treaty	signed agreement between two or more nations

British soldiers in 1915, taking a break during the fighting in Turkey.

However, during a career in the government that lasted for more than 60 years, Churchill made mistakes.

Too sure of himself?

Earlier in his career, during World War I (1914–1918), Churchill planned a military attack in Turkey in 1915. Over 250,000 British, French, New Zealand, and Australian troops died in the failed attack. Critics claimed that Churchill had been too sure of himself and risked too much.

Many experts believe that Churchill's greatest weakness was his self-confidence. He wanted to be at the centre of things and be in charge. Even when others doubted him, Churchill remained confident about his decisions.

Does a leader need such extreme self-confidence? How can a leader know if he or she is making the right decisions?

Leading fact!

Churchill even learned to fly an aeroplane, but he crashed it twice in one day!

This photograph of Churchill was taken during World War I at the time of the fighting in Turkey.

Richard Nixon

(1913–1994)

Richard Nixon was US president from 1969 to 1974. In the late 1960s, people feared the possibility of nuclear war. Such a war could mean the end of the world.

Treaties and trade

Nixon met with Leonid Brezhnev, leader of the **Soviet Union**, to reduce the possibility of nuclear war. They helped create **treaties** that calmed people's fears.

Nixon also visited China. There was no trade or business between China and the United States before Nixon's visit. Afterwards, relationships improved. Some people believe that Nixon's actions in 1972 created the lively trade programme that now exists between the United States and China.

nuclear war	**war using weapons powered by nuclear energy**
Soviet Union	**nation that consisted of several countries that joined together from 1922 to 1991**

Nixon (centre) with China's leader, Zhou Enlai (left), in 1972.

Leading fact!

By 2006 China was the world's third-largest exporter (seller) of trade goods. Its economy is expected to continue to grow by 9 per cent a year.

Richard Nixon (right) leaves the White House for good. With him are Vice President Ford, Mrs. Ford, and Mrs. Nixon.

However, around 2:30 a.m. on 17 June 1972, five men broke into the Watergate Building in Washington, D.C., and installed hidden cameras in the **Democratic Party** headquarters. When the men were arrested, they said they worked for President Nixon's re-election committee. Were they planning to spy on the Democrats, Nixon's opponents?

Did he know?

Nixon said he knew nothing about the break-in, but the American people did not believe him. Nixon had been accused of such tricks before.

Americans were ashamed of Nixon. They no longer wanted him as their president. On 9 August 1974, Richard Nixon became the only US president ever to **resign** from office.

Nixon felt that the laws did not apply to him because he was the president. Should leaders have to obey the same laws as everyone else? Should leaders be forgiven if they make mistakes?

Democratic Party one of two major political parties in the United States. The other is the Republican Party.

resign to give up an office or position

You Decide

What do you think of the leaders in this book? Do you see them as "heroes" or "zeros"?

Consider this:

Joan of Arc claimed that she had never personally killed anyone. However, as the leader of an army, was she responsible for the deaths they caused?

When Winston Churchill died at the age of 90, a reporter noted, "He [Churchill] was never afraid to lead, and he knew that a leader must sometimes risk failure and disapproval." Are there times when a leader should take action, whether or not people approve? Are there times when a leader should have the people's approval before acting?

What qualities does a good leader have?

If a world leader came to you looking for advice, what would you say?

Which world leader do you most admire? Why?

Nations honour their leaders and heroes by printing their faces on money. Which leader would you have on your bank notes?

Glossary

ambitious eagerly desiring success, power, and wealth. Nixon was an ambitious man.

convert change from one religion to another

Democratic Party one of two major political parties in the United States. The other is the Republican Party.

dictator ruler with absolute (unquestioned) power

empire group of nations under the same ruler

Inquisition search for non-believers. The Spanish Inquisition began in 1480 in Castile, Spain.

inquisitor official investigator. Joan of Arc was questioned by an inquisitor.

Napoleonic Code system of law based on Roman law. Many countries base their laws on the Napoleonic Code.

nuclear war war using weapons powered by nuclear energy

Parliament group of elected people who make laws

prime minister head of the government in a country with a parliament. Winston Churchill served twice as prime minister.

resign to give up an office or position. Nixon was the only US president to resign.

saint person recognized by the Catholic Church as having great holiness. Many people call Joan of Arc "Saint Joan".

senator (in ancient Rome) person who helped to make the laws

Soviet Union nation that consisted of several countries that joined together from 1922 to 1991. The Soviet Union split into many different nations, including Russia, in 1991.

treaty signed agreement between two or more nations

Want to know more?

Books

- *Julius Caesar: Great Dictator of Rome*, Richard Platt (Dorling Kindersley, 2006) (Reprint edition)
- *Napoleon Bonaparte and Imperial France*, Miriam Greenblatt (Benchmark Books, 2006)
- *Ten Queens: Portraits of Women of Power*, Milton Meltzer (Dutton Children's Books, 2003) (Reprint edition)
- *Winston Churchill*, Simon Adams (Raintree, 2003)

Websites

- www.roman-empire.net/children/index.html
- www.napoleon.org/en/fun_stuff/puzzles/index.asp
  Assemble an e-jigsaw puzzle of Napoleon.

If you liked this Atomic book, why don't you try these...?

Index

Notes for adults
Use the following questions to guide children towards identifying features of report text:

Can you find an example of a general opening classification on page 4?
Can you give an example of a generic participant on page 7?
Can you find examples of the details of an owl's night vision on page 15?
Can you find examples of non-chronological language on page 23?
Can you give examples of present tense language on page 27?